The Little Turner

Catherine de Duve

KATE'ART EDITIONS

IN TURNER'S

Turner

In Turner's day, around the time he was born, many changes and events would impact life in England and the whole of Europe.

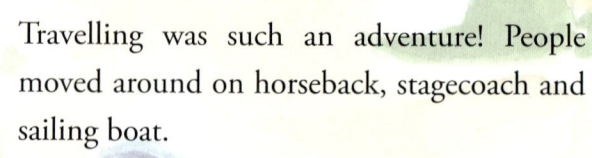

Travelling was such an adventure! People moved around on horseback, stagecoach and sailing boat.

A stagecoach, caught in a snowstorm in the night.

Sailing boat

London, around 1809

TIMES

It was the Industrial Revolution in England. Factories and machines were being built. Railway lines and steamboats made their first appearance in the landscape.

Steam engine

The French Revolution began in 1789. The king and queen were decapitated! It was also the beginning of the War of Independence in America and the war between France and England.

Steamboat

Napoleon became French Emperor in 1804 and wanted to conquer the world!

Napoleon

TURNER

The Turner family lived close to Covent Garden in London. Joseph Mallord William Turner was born on 23rd April 1775. As a child, he loved to draw. His father was a barber and a wigmaker. "One day my son will be an artist!", he used to tell his clients. And by 12, the young Turner was already exhibiting and selling his drawings in the family shop.

Turner spent part of his childhood outside London because his mother was slowly but surely going insane. He did not go to school much and so could not write or speak very well.

Who was Turner?
He was short, had a big nose and a hoarse voice. He had terrible fits of rage. Here, he painted himself in a flattering way.

Turner was eccentric and secretive. To this day, we know very little about his private life. He never married but had two daughters. Turner loved living by the Thames and also spent quite a lot of time travelling around England to paint. His favourite hobby? Fishing!

Heron

Find the pike that Turner caught.
How about you? What's your favourite hobby?

5

THE ROYAL ACADEMY

When Turner was 14 he decided to become a full-time painter. In order to learn his craft he copied and studied the works of past masters that he discovered at Dr Monro's, his mother's doctor. Turner also painted "topographical" watercolours for an architect. He was very talented!

Topographical watercolours: : In those days there weren't any photographs or postcards. In order to get a faithful reproduction of a landscape, people asked artists to paint watercolours which use water based paints on paper. Engravings were then made from these and printed in books as illustrations.

Look at this engraving. It is a copy of a watercolour by Turner. Can you describe the scene? Do you prefer drawing or taking a picture of a place?

Turner's entire life was dedicated to his work. He attracted patrons who helped him gain entry to the Royal Academy, the prestigious art school. It was also renowned for exhibitions. Years later he became professor of perspective and a member of the prestigious new institution presided over by the painter Reynolds (1723-1792). Turner also exhibited his watercolours there, and in 1796, for the first time, he showed an oil painting: *Fishermen at Sea*.

Moonlight

Turner painted the moonlight emphasising light and colour. Look at the painting with care. What time of day is it? Where does the scene take place? How is it lit?

PAINTER OF LIGHT

Turner travelled through the English counties and drew the landscape. He was preparing a book. He painted this painting by a river on the Scottish border in 1797. Turner painted the same landscape approximately 50 years later! His style had changed completely. His later paintings are hazy and look unfinished, the light soft. He was nicknamed the painter of light. He did not hesitate to paint with his fingers. In those times no one painted like that!

Norham Castle, 1797

Around 1845

Compare the two different ways of painting the same landscape. Which do you prefer? Which is the most precise? Find the castle, the sun, the mountains and the cows.

AVALANCHE

Beware the avalanche! The enormous amount of moving snow takes with it boulders and blocs of ice, violently ripping up pine trees and crushing a small refuge. Turner wrote: "And towering glaciers fall, the work of ages crashing through all!" He often added verse to his exhibited works drawing out moral points. Here he is depicting how man is powerless when face to face with the forces of nature.

How do you feel when you look at this painting?

Technique: To express the violence of the avalanche, Turner used his palette knife. He spread the white paint on the canvas structuring the facets of ice with the knife.

In 1802, thanks to a short-lived peace between France and England, Turner was finally able to cross the Channel. He set foot on the continent for the first time in Calais on his way to Switzerland. The trip was full of danger but the landscape was completely different to that of his own country. The mountains, the precipices and the glaciers fired the painter's imagination.

TURNER AND

On his way back from Switzerland, Turner stayed in Paris for two days to discover the Louvre, recently made a national museum. Napoleon had brought back vast treasures from his conquests! The English painter could study the works of great masters there. His ambition? To surpass them. Turner admired the paintings of French artists of the 18th century, in particular those of Claude, known as le Lorrain, and Nicolas Poussin.
In those times, artists read classical writings in Greek and Latin and painted historic scenes showing characters from the Bible and mythology.

Mythology: A set of widely held but exaggerated or fictitious stories or beliefs sometimes used to explain natural phenomena such as storms or the birth of cities.

THE GREAT MASTERS

The sun rises over the prosperous town of Carthage in Africa. Queen Dido supervises the work. The architects show their plans, the masons go about their work, and the merchandise is unloaded. Next to the shipyard, children play with small boats. Can you see them?

The National Gallery opened in 1824. Turner donated this painting under one condition: that it be hung next to the work of his master, Claude.

Compare Claude Lorrain's painting with Turner's below.

MARITIME ART

The boats are sinking. The sailors are swept away by huge waves. One of them sounds the alarm with a bugle. Help! Can you hear it? Are there any survivors?

Turner, The Shipwreck (oil on canvas)

Look closely at the engraving and the oil painting.

A Shipwreck (engraving)

During his visit to the Louvre, Turner was impressed by the seascapes of great Dutch painters. He painted *The Shipwreck* and had 50 engravings made of it. It was a great success! It was the first oil painting Turner made into an engraving.

Compare Turner's seascapes with those of the Dutch painters of the 18th century.

Van Ruisdael

Van de Velde the Young

Turner

MY ART GALLERY

In 1804, Turner was 29 years old. He was already very successful and opened an art gallery in his London home at 64, Harley Street. He exhibited his work there permanently.

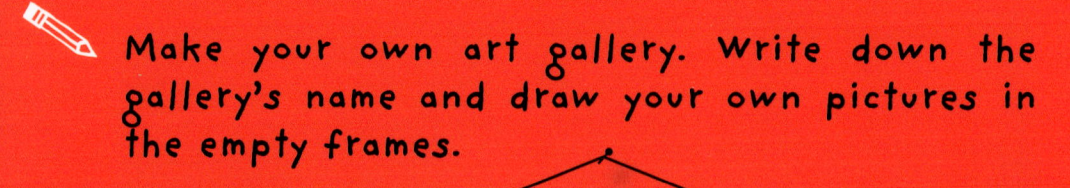

Make your own art gallery. Write down the gallery's name and draw your own pictures in the empty frames.

Gallery

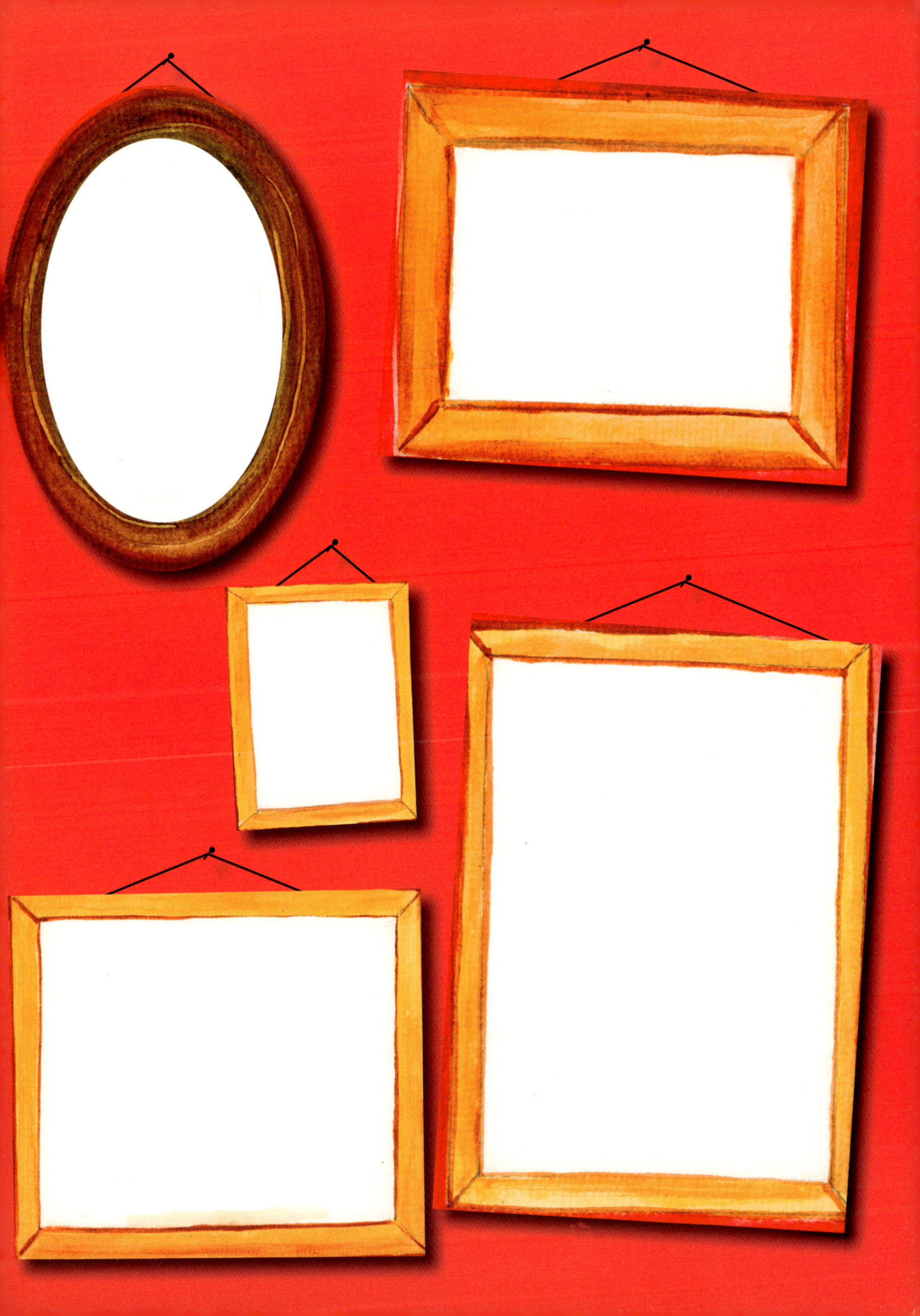

TRAFALGAR

Admiral Nelson

Napoleon was determined to annihilate the English fleet that was stopping him from ruling the seas. On 21st October 1805, a terrible naval battle raged at the Cape of Trafalgar, off the Spanish coast. The British Royal Navy had 27 vessels. Nelson was on board the three-masted flagship, the H.M.S. *Victory*, with her 104 cannons. On raising the ship's colours, the admiral declared: "England expects that every man will do his duty." The adversaries were 33 allied French and Spanish ships; 22 were lost in battle. No English ships were lost but Nelson died a hero. When the *Victory* returned to England, Turner boarded the ship, talked to the crew and drew a sketch of the deck.

Find these details in the battle scene.

Nelson

The French flag

Smoke from the cannons

A few years later, Turner painted his favourite canvas. The Fighting *Temeraire* was a veteran gunship of Trafalgar. Here she is, ghostlike, tugged by a steamboat to her last berth to be broken up.

Look at the colours of the painting.

Goethe's *Theory of Colours* influenced Turner. The way he used blue and orange paints in this picture creates a grandiose effect. The old ship is painted in muted tones and is illuminated by a triangle of blue sky, whereas the steam-driven black tugboat, a symbol of progress, moves proudly towards us. Can you see the vessels?

TRAVEL JOURNALS

Whilst travelling widely, Turner drew tirelessly in homemade notebooks. Lakes, mountains, castles, cities... He was asked to illustrate travel journals aimed at the earliest tourists.

Lake Lucerne

Draw in your travel journal just like Turner did. Remember to write the date, the name of the place you've sketched and your impressions; you can even write a poem.

Lake Como

Plymouth

Paris

Prague

Gulf of Naples

VENICE

The Napoleonic wars prevented Turner from travelling to the continent again. Only when he was 44 years old could he finally go to Italy. Italy! It was a destination for all artists who wanted to mature under the influence of *classical art* and the particular light there. The English painter visited Turin, Como, Venice, Florence, Rome and Naples. Here he is in Venice…

Classical art *represents the ideal of beauty for artists who inspired themselves from ancient and Roman art rediscovered during the Renaissance.*

Turner

22

Turner was fascinated by the light in Venice and the clear blue skies above the city. He began to use increasingly bright colours. One hundred years earlier, the Venetian painter Canaletto (1697-1768) had already depicted views of his city with great precision.

Compare the work of Turner and Canaletto. What similarities are there? Find the gondolas, the dogs, the merchants, customs and the church domes.

Canaletto

FIRE!

During the night of 16th October 1834, Westminster Palace was in flames. This was the seat of Parliament, of both the House of Lords and the House of Commons. Londoners massed in boats, on bridges and along the River Thames all fascinated by the spectacular fire. Where was Turner? He wouldn't miss such an event for anything.

🔍 Look at these two versions painted by Turner. Which seems the most impressive to you?

Later, in his studio, he recalled the burning of Parliament. He painted several versions from different perspectives. He imagined also the dramatic fire, which in 475 reduced the library in Constantinople to cinders.

The burning of Constantinople

STORM AT SEA

Here is the *Ariel*, a steamship battling against the savage elements. The ship, caught in a tempest, sends out a distress signal. Turner explained to visitors to his gallery that he was tied to the mast of the ship for four hours to better observe the stormy seas. True or false?

Throughout his life, Turner loved to paint the sea, the light, the wind, fishermen as well as progress. At that time, the steamboat began to make an appearance in paintings.

And you? What new things would you paint in the landscape today?

LOCOMOTIVE

At that time in England, steam trains made their appearance with railways, viaducts and bridges. They transformed the countryside. Travelling became faster and less dangerous. Turner believed in progress.

🔍 **Find in the painting the viaduct, the hare, a labourer and a fishing boat. Do you know which is the fastest locomotive in the world?**

The Firefly Class steam locomotive was one of the most modern at the time. It could travel at 70 miles per hour, a record! Here is the one belonging to the Great Western Railway. It is travelling at great speed in the rain and crosses the new bridge at Maidenhead over the Thames. Choo! Choo! All aboard for Bristol! In the foreground of the picture a terrified hare bounds away from the terrible din of the engine. Which of the two goes the fastest?

THE FINAL TOUCHES

A few days before the opening of an exhibition, artists used to add the finishing touches to their paintings. They also applied the final layer of varnish (*vernis*). That is why the opening of an exhibition is called the *vernissage*. So the openings or *vernissages*, became social occasions for members of the Royal Academy.

In 1832 one of Turner's pictures was hung next to a large coloured canvas painted by Constable (1776-1837). Turner's painting was a small seascape. After having looked at his painting in its new environment for a long time, he added a small red dash in the sea. The following day he returned and transformed the red dash into a buoy. Can you see it? Turner loved to challenge his contemporaries.

Find the red buoy in the painting.

At the end of his career, Turner exposed canvases that were little more than sketches. People no longer understood him and mocked him: "This gentleman has […] chosen to paint with cream, or chocolate, yoke of egg, or currant jelly." Others admired him. This was the case of Ruskin, a well-known art critic, who defended Turner's work, considering him a great master.

Joseph Mallord William Turner passed away on the evening of 19th December 1851 in Chelsea. He was buried according to his wishes in St Paul's Cathedral in London.

Text and illustration: Catherine de Duve
Graphic design: Kate'Art Editions
Concept and coordination: Kate'Art Editions & Happy Museum!
Translation: Kerry-Jane Lowery

Photographic credits:

London: Tate: *Self-Portrait*, 1799: cover, p.1, p.4 - *London*, around 1809: p.2 - *War. The Exile and the Rock Limpet*, 1842: p.3 - *Peace-Burial at Sea*, 1842: p.3 - *Fishermen at Sea*, 1796: p.7 - *Norham Castle*, 1797: p.9 - *Norham Castle, Sunrise*, c.1845-1850: cover, p.8-9 - *The Fall of an Avalanche in the Grisons*, 1810: p.10 - *The Shipwreck*, 1805: p.14 - *The Battle of Trafalgar*, 1806: p.18 - *Lake Como*, 1819: p.21 - *A Town on a River at Sunset, c.1833*: p.21 - *The Convent on the Rock, after Richard Wilson*, 1796-7: p.21 - *Naples vue de Capodimonte*, 1819: p.21 - *Paris: The Pont Neuf and the Ile de la Cité*, c.1833: p.21 - *The Dogana, San Giorgio, Citella, From the Steps of the Europa*, 1842: p.22 - *Snow Storm - Steam-Boat off a Harbour's Mouth Making Signals in Shallow Water, and Going by the Lead. The author was in the storm on the night the Ariel left Harwich*, 1842: p.26-27 - *Cockermouth Castle*, c.1830: p.30 - **National Gallery:** Turner: *Dido Building Carthage; or, Rise of the Carthaginian Empire.-1ˢᵗ Book of Virgil's Aeneid*,1815: p.13 - *Dutch Boats in a Gale*, 1801: p.15 - *The Fighting Temeraire*, 1839: cover, p.19 - *Rain, Steam and Speed – The Great Western Railway, 1844*: cover, p.2, p.28-29 - Claude Lorrain: *Seaport with the Embarkation of the Queen of Sheba, 1648*: p.12 - **British Museum:** *Messieurs les voyageurs*, 1829: p.2 - Charles Turner: A Shipwreck, 1806: p.14 - Abbott: **National Maritime Museum, London. Greenwich Hospital Collection:** *Contre-amiral Sir Horacio Nelson*, 1800: p.18 - **Paul Mellon Centre for Studies in British Art:** J.E. Millais, *Vernissage Morning at the Royal Academy*, 1851: p.30 - **Paris, Réunion des musées nationaux:** Turner: *The Burning of Constantinople, n.d.*: p.25 - H. Lewandowski, G.Blot/C.Jean, T. Le Mage
USA: Turner: **Indianapolis Museum of Art:** *Self-Portrait*, 1792: p.2 - **The Frick collection (New York):** *Cologne: The Arrival of a Packet-Boat: Evening*, 1826: p. 2 - **Philadelphia Museum of Art:** *The Burning of the Houses of Lords and Commons, October 16, 1834*, 1834-35: p.24 - **The Cleveland Museum of Art:** *The Burning of the Houses of Lords and Commons, October 16, 1834*, 1835: p.25 - Van de Velde the Younger: **Toledo Museum of Art:** *A Rising Gale*, c. 1672: p.15 - Van Ruisdael: **Kimbell Art Museum (Texas):** *Rough Sea at a Jetty*, 1650: p.15 - Canaletto: **National Gallery of Washington, D.C.:** *Entrance to the Grand Canal from the Molo, Venice*, 1742-44: p.23 -
Tokyo: Fuji Art Museum: Turner: *Helvoetsluys - Le « Ville d'Utrecht », 64, prenant la mer*, 1832: p.31
- **Collection privée:** *Heron with a Fish, n.d.*: p.5 - *View of Plymouth*, 1813: p.21 - Comte d'Orsay, *Turner à la « Conversazione » de Elhanan, Bickwell*, 1850 - *The Blue Rigi: Lake of Lucerne*, 1842: p.20

With thanks to: Dorine Devosse, Clair O'Leary, Tate, Daniel de Duve, Priscilla d'Oultremont, Edition Le Cri and everyone who helped to make this book.